SET FREE

Why I Am Not Ashamed of the Gospel of Jesus Christ

REVISED EDITION

SET FREE

**Why I Am Not Ashamed of
the Gospel of Jesus Christ**

REVISED EDITION

Peter A. Rahme

SET FREE

Why I Am Not Ashamed of
the Gospel of Jesus Christ

Cover Design and Interior Layout by Uberwriters
www.uberwriters.com

Unless otherwise indicated, scripture quotations taken from the New King James Version®. Copyright © 1982 by Thomas Nelson. Used by permission. All rights reserved.

Scripture quotations marked (AMP) are taken from the Amplified® Bible (AMP), Copyright © 2015 by The Lockman Foundation. Used by permission. www.Lockman.org.

Scripture quotations marked (CJB) are taken from the Complete Jewish Bible by David H. Stern. Copyright © 1998. All rights reserved. Used by permission of Messianic Jewish Publishers, 6120 Day Long Lane, Clarksville, MD 21029. www.messianicjewish.net.

ISBN paperback: 978-0-9996668-4-5
ISBN eBook: 978-0-9996668-5-2

Peter Rahme Ministries
P.O Box 851, Prospect, KY 40059, USA
www.CompelThem.com

Contents

Acknowledgements

To my precious wife, Dyllis, for her astounding character, integrity, and endurance in sticking with me through the bad times and the good. I love you, my lady.

And to my amazing sons, Hilton, Grant, and Bradley, for helping me with this book.

Chapter One
The Early Years

A Careless, Drunken Fool

As my brother filled his car with gas, I saw a man gesturing to my wife and sister-in-law out of the corner of my eye. I sat in the passenger's seat while my embarrassed wife and her sister were chatting in the rear seat when this man began his unwelcome behavior. I casually called the guy over, not really expecting him to respond, but he was drunk, so he foolishly strolled over to my side of the car. As he approached, I opened the window and pulled out a small pistol I had been carrying for my sister-in-law. Unfortunately, I, too, was drunk.

When the guy bent down to the window, I put the loaded pistol to his head and pulled the trigger. I was surprised when no bullet was discharged and pulled the trigger again. The man's eyes suddenly widened, realizing what had just happened, then he turned and fled in terror.

Confused (knowing nothing about firearms at the time), I asked my sister-in-law why the gun hadn't fired. "You have to take the safety catch off," she replied. I found the safety, flipped it off, and pulled the trigger again. This time the pistol blasted a round through the car's window with a loud bang, and we all jumped. Thankfully, nobody was hurt . . . or killed.

To this day, I have a constant reminder of my foolish, reckless, drunken behavior—tinnitus, a relentless ringing in my left ear. This was the tip of the iceberg of what I put my wife through, often while drunk.

Jeppestown

To give you a little background of my very impressionable childhood, my dad bought a grocery and convenience store when I was six. This store was in a suburb of Johannesburg, South Africa, called Jeppestown. Jeppestown (or Jeppe as it is commonly known) is about fifteen miles from the center of downtown Johannesburg and was home to some of the most violent, careless, and heartless people one can imagine. Little has changed. On the 25th of June, 2006, "The

Jeppestown Tragedy," as it is known, involved a crazy shootout between local law enforcement and a large gang of armed robbers. During the gunfight, four police officers and eight robbers were killed before the remaining fifteen gang members surrendered.

This gives you some insight into what my family and I had to deal with for eleven years in Jeppe.

My dad's store was broken into thirteen times in eleven years and was thoroughly cleaned out each time. We packaged our own sugar, flour, rice, etc., from 100 and 200-lb. sacks we kept in storage. Every time they burgled the store, these criminals would rip every sack open, empty the contents onto the floor in the middle of the store, and anything that wasn't nailed down was packed into the sacks. Reliable neighborhood sources told us who had robbed us, but these criminals offered a piece of their pie to anyone who could identify them to keep them from talking to the police. It wouldn't have even mattered because the police were too scared to investigate, knowing they, and their families, would be targeted.

During these difficult years, my dad, my brothers, and I had to fight these deranged criminals off regularly. We were a peace-loving family, but we were tough too. We had to be. When my dad was about sixty years old, one of the most violent, tattoo-covered ex-jailbirds walked into our store, swearing and being extremely rowdy and obnoxious. We could smell the booze from across the store, so we knew he was looking for a fight. Just minutes before, he had savagely beaten a defenseless black man who had been innocently walking by the store. My dad asked him to be quiet, and he said something disrespectful to my dad. Then my mom told him to leave, and he swore at my mother this time.

Now, my dad was a very even-tempered man, but if there was ever a way to rouse my dad's anger, it was to disrespect my mother. Even I, and any one of my nine siblings, knew better than to do this. My dad quietly walked to the store's front doors and locked them. He then rolled up his sleeves and focused on the giant troublemaker.

That day my dad taught this hoodlum the lesson of his life! Although my dad was only about 5' 6" tall, he was as broad as a barn door. He was nicknamed "Jack" after the renowned world heavyweight boxing champion Jack Dempsey.

That was one of a handful of stories from Jeppe that had a mildly happy ending. Most didn't. In my youth, we saw stabbings, crazy, brutal fights, sometimes even between fathers and sons, and once a man even took an axe to his wife, killing her. As children, we saw gruesome cock fights, dog fights, and various other atrocities. Still, the most vivid and horrific memory I have was witnessing some of these wicked guys throw a man off a high train bridge—the fall instantly killing him.

Once these evil men had left, I remember running up to where he had been thrown off and looking down from the bridge at the man's broken body, lying disjointed across the train lines. No one—least of all a child—should ever have to witness such violent and devilish crimes.

The saddest part is that cycles seem to perpetuate themselves. The forces of evil are reluctant to give up their quest for the souls of men, and children filled with fear at such a young age so often end up emulating the horrible things they've been exposed to.

For eleven years, I was surrounded by and immersed in this lifestyle, and eventually, I succumbed to the same evil. I learned to gamble, swear, smoke marijuana, drink, and fight like these vicious, violent men. What I hated with a passion, I saw myself becoming.

The Boat

By the time I was eighteen, my brothers and our friends had a reputation to be feared. One night my brother, four friends, and I were at a local nightclub called The Boat. When we got inside, we saw about thirty guys from the other side of town who considered us their arch-enemies.

The hostility between the two groups was tangible, and within minutes chaos broke out. The other group jumped up suddenly and attacked us with broken bottles, chairs, and knives. We fought valiantly, but we were outnumbered five to one. My cousin and a friend of ours had bottles smashed in their faces, and others in our group were struck with chains across their backs. Then it got worse.

My brother Patrick was viciously stabbed twice—the first blade penetrating six inches into his back. His thick, leather belt was cut in half as another knife sliced through it, sinking into his lower back and creating a nine-inch wound.

Then it was my turn.

The cowards preferred stabbing from behind, so I, too, was stabbed in the back. The knife plunged through my back, between my ribs, and into my torso. When the fight was over, I lost track of my brother and my friends, so I walked several miles home with blood streaming down my back. My eldest brother sped me to the hospital in his car, where they took x-rays. The nurse told me the blade missed my heart by only half an inch.

Death Bend

Another time, five friends and I drove around town while drinking heavily and completely out of control. We heard sirens a few blocks away and soon saw a police chase taking place right before us (it wasn't the first time). The police were in pursuit of some gangsters, and for some reason, we decided it would be a great idea to chase the police.

As my friend accelerated to crazy speeds trying to keep up with the police car, we approached a hairpin turn aptly named "Death Bend." We were going so fast there wasn't the slightest chance we'd make the turn. The car smashed into the barrier, careening into a crazy death roll. The car was going so fast it flipped over eight times and knocked out several metal safety poles. As we spun through the air, with the metal, glass, and pavement crashing all around me, I remember shouting a full-throated cry: "Please, God, let us land on our wheels!" Almost instantly, we did, and the car bounced and rolled to a stop. Miraculously, nobody was seriously injured.

You'd think we'd all be literally scared sober, but with the ingratitude and rebellion of youthful waywardness, we all laughed madly, shouting and cheering out of our wrecked (but somehow drivable) car, with all the windows smashed out. We continued partying into the night, which was the way I lived. I had no idea at the time it was completely unsustainable.

Accused Number One

My life began to get uglier and uglier. What should have been a happy day of celebration when a friend got married instead turned into a nasty confrontation with the police. With too much alcohol flowing and tempers rising at the wedding, a huge fight broke out with some outsiders. Our clan was somewhat notorious at this point, so the police were quickly called.

When the police arrived, they were in no mood to ask questions, and we were in no mood to stop fighting. In the ensuing pandemonium, I broke a colonel's jaw. For my reward, three policemen pinned my arms behind my back, while a fourth shattered my nose.

Once subdued, I was unceremoniously thrown into the back of a police van. In the prior mayhem, I tried to help my brother Patrick, who was paralytic drunk. The irony was that my brother, Ronald, had been trying to help me and get me away from the fight with the police. With Patrick and me out of the way, several police officers turned their attention to my relatively innocent brother, Ronald. They surrounded him and managed to beat him down, then two policemen dragged him through the streets like a dog. This sight filled me with a blinding rage, and I snapped.

The side window of the police van was covered with a heavy mesh about an eighth inch thick and secured with solid rivets about four inches apart. In a maniacal fury, I punched my fingers into the mesh and ripped it clean off the rivets. As the rivets popped from the van frame, it sounded like someone was firing a machine gun.

I opened the window to climb through, and as I put my head out, I stared down the barrel of a double-action Walther P38 9mm pistol. A policeman was waiting for me, grinning icily as he nodded and said, "Go ahead. Please." I reluctantly withdrew into the van and sat down, my heart pounding, blood still pouring from my nose.

I spent the weekend in a jail cell, and the following Monday morning, everyone who had been arrested was put on trial. The officers made sure I was accused number one out of the six of us being charged. The Lord had been watching over me even back then because only He knows how I was acquitted.

This was just one of the countless incidents that brought distress and despair to my beautiful wife and children.

Darkest before the Dawn

I wish I could say it wasn't the case, but I pointed a pistol at yet another man with lethal intent; that man was me. There were several times during my life when I became severely suicidal. During these moments of despair and hopelessness, I found myself pointing my .45 Colt pistol at my own head, closing my eyes and shaking as I fought myself to not pull the trigger.

By that point, it felt as if I was controlled by an evil force or spirit that kept telling me over and over, "Take your life. There is nothing to live for!" This dreadful voice was obviously lying to me, as I had a beautiful wife and three fantastic young sons. I had a lot to live for, but the lifestyle and deception I'd opened myself up to was robbing me of everything!

Being a Catholic, I was taught that if you take your own life, you will not enter the Kingdom of Heaven. This terrified me as I believed if I pulled the trigger, I would be on my way to hell for all eternity! I suppose it was a good thing at the time. At that low point in my life, I lived on a roller coaster. I spent my time stoned or high on a cocktail of recreational drugs. After coming down from a high, I would shake with paranoid fear, then have to get high again to feel the slightest sense of peace. Over and over, I repeated this cycle, and each time I kept crying out louder and louder, "If there is a God out there, I want to know You. If Jesus is Your Son, I need Him, and I need You."I want to pause a moment in the story because I believe it's important for you to recognize a vital truth—you are reading this book for a reason. I think you must understand how I reached this dire and dangerous stage of my life. By this point, I had been addicted to hard drugs for fourteen years and drinking copious amounts of alcohol for twenty years. I had also been smoking hashish for over twenty-five years—from the tender age of nine! Finally, I reached the point where I was totally reckless, careless, and living only for myself and whatever I could get out of life.

It didn't start that way, of course—out of boredom and bad neighborhood influences, I initially decided to try something new, believing I could never get hooked by any drug or alcohol.

Don't ever be fooled—you could get hooked from the first moment! What may appear harmless fun opens the door to total dependency and a path of self-destruction. Many people allow themselves to be pressured by peers into trying a new drug or just having one drink. Believe me, it's not worth it.

Protecting Angels

During these reckless years, I was involved in three near-fatal car accidents. On one occasion, I was speeding along a highway at a harrowing eighty miles per hour when I approached the top of a blind rise in the road. As I crested the hill, suddenly, another car was directly in front of me on the wrong side of the road. With a sickening, deafening crunch, our vehicles collided head-on.

The driver of the other vehicle was horribly drunk. Thankfully, my wife and children were at home—leaving them behind so I could join friends to party on vacation. Unfortunately, my car was totaled instead. To this day, I have no doubt there is any way I could have survived that wreckage without divine intervention.

You'd think events like that would wake me up to my mortality, but life continued to spiral; downward. I was shot at several times—bullets narrowly missing me and had guns pointed at me more than once. By this point, I worked as a gun dealer and had amassed seventeen firearms of my own.

In another stabbing, I was knifed through the hand while protecting my face from a murderous attack. The blade severed my tendon, and to this day, my hand has limited use.

Something had to change, as it was just a matter of time before I was killed or killed myself. I knew my days were shortly numbered if something didn't change, as did my wife. Every time I went out, she waited in despair for the phone call or the knock at the door confirming I had finally been killed.

Chapter Two

A Rebel in Need of Truth

In late South-African autumn, things came to a head. My sister asked me to attend a Christian meeting with her, so on the 26th of May, 1980, I walked into a church service to please her. It was a Monday evening, and I took my wife and three sons with me, not wanting to go on my own. I knew the minister preaching that night, as he was a Lebanese friend of my brother-in-law and sister. At the end of the service, he asked the congregation if anyone would like to invite Jesus Christ into their heart and make Him their Lord and Savior. Nobody raised a hand, and I could feel everyone in the service focusing on me. I did stick out like a sore thumb, with my hair hanging almost to my waist and my thick beard halfway down my chest. Being one of the pioneers of South Africa's hippy movement (albeit with little peace, love, and flowers), I wore a pair of skintight Levi jeans, a red-and-white plaid shirt, thick blue suspenders, and a pair of worn-out western boots. Who wouldn't have focused on me?

The minister said, "There is a man here God is speaking to. If he doesn't come forward tonight, he could end up in much more trouble." Knowing nothing about a prophetic word from the Holy Spirit, and with my heart still rebellious and stubborn, I muttered under my breath, "God knows you're talking to me . . . I know it, and the devil knows it! Now, get off my back," and I promptly took my family and walked out of the service. But something powerful had already happened to me that night. In my heart, I knew those people had something I didn't—something I desperately needed. But instead of acknowledging this, I responded in my typically defiant way.

At this point, I hadn't worked for seven months. Every morning at about 6:00 a.m. I would make myself a hash joint, drop a few pills, and ease into my day. This had been my routine for many years. At about 8:00 a.m. every morning, once my wife had gone to work and my children were at school, my personal pub in the fridge would open, and I would start drinking.

I wasn't only a drug addict but an alcoholic as well. This enslaved lifestyle had me in bondage to great confusion and contributed to the constant violence, hatred, and enmity surrounding me.

The world was spinning too fast, and I couldn't keep up, so all I wanted to do was jump off. I honestly believed the only way out was to take my life.

Rejoice, for I Have Delivered You

The morning after walking out of the church service, when I had refused to accept Jesus Christ as my Lord and Savior, I fell into a deep depression. Having openly defied a warning by the minister and rejected accepting Jesus Christ, I knew I was now definitely bound for hell. A sinister voice began repeating the same words over and over: "Anyone who takes LSD will *never* enter the Kingdom of Heaven." I had no idea the devil is the father of all lies, as Jesus tells us in John 8:44. Ironically, the same voice would say at other times, "There is no Kingdom of Heaven!" I had grown up with some knowledge of Christ, so in my rebellion and confusion after walking out of that service, I knew I was a sure candidate for hell, which utterly terrified me.

Trying to escape these intrusive thoughts, I wandered aimlessly around the house and into the backyard, feeling anxious and terribly convicted of all my sins. Interestingly, I was so depressed

I couldn't even bring myself to take any pills or pour a drink.

Our Will Can Override God's Will in Our Lives

Just before noon on the 27th of May, 1980, a sunny autumn Tuesday morning, I forced myself to make a joint. On that pivotal day, I saw just how powerful the will of an individual truly is. In fact, I learned firsthand my personal will was even stronger than God's will in my life. I hadn't taken three drags of the joint when all hell broke loose in my mind. I somehow glimpsed a spiritual war that was raging for my very soul. I was so freaked out I immediately ran to the kitchen, thinking I needed a strong drink, or even a cup of coffee, to calm my nerves.

As I reached the kitchen, something was different, something inexplicable. It was much brighter than before. I switched the kettle on to make some coffee. With my hands still trembling like leaves in a storm, I tried to add a spoonful of instant coffee into my cup but missed it completely, spilling coffee granules onto the floor. I had never felt this way—I was shaking uncontrollably for no apparent reason. I knew it wasn't the few small drags on the joint—I had smoked ten times that much with little effect, and even LSD and other hard drugs had never affected me in this way.

Totally confused and panicking, my heart pounded nearly out of my chest. As I battled to regain some form of composure, I noticed the sweetest harmony of voices on the radio. It was a song I had never heard before, and the lyrics almost blew my mind:

Come with me, down paradise road

This way please, I'll carry your load

This you won't believe.

Come with me to paradise skies

Look outside and open your eyes

This you must believe.

There are better days before us

And a burning bridge behind, fire smokin' the sky is blazing,

There's a woman waiting weeping

And a young man nearly beaten all for love.

Paradise was almost closin' down.

Come with me to paradise days

It'll change your life, it'll sure change your ways

This you won't believe.

Take my hand down paradise lane

Away from heartache without any pain

I know 'cause I have been.

There are better days before us

And a burning bridge behind, fire smokin', the sky is blazing . . .

The song was amazingly called "Paradise Road[1]" by a South African group called Joy. Although they weren't Christian at the time, the lyrics shook me to the core. The message was Heaven-sent smack in the middle of my personal war between good and evil, life and eternal death.

Because the song spoke about paradise and how it would "change your life" and would "sure change your ways," it ignited in my heart desperately needed hope that there would be "better days before us" for me personally and in our strife-torn nation. I'll never forget the angelic sound of this beautiful song on that special day. *If God can use a song on the radio timed perfectly for my crisis, perhaps Heaven isn't out of reach for me.*

Suddenly my kitchen was lit up with the glory of God—it was so bright even the noonday sun seemed dull in comparison. Yet, I still truly did not know if I would live or die. With the war raging in my mind, I was so fearful it even crossed my thoughts that God might kill me. At this point, I began to cry and sprinted out of the kitchen to the bathroom, unsure of why I was running. As I did, I felt myself being drawn back into the brightness and glory in the kitchen, but I resisted, still terrified of the supernatural event taking place in my life.

Then I heard these words: "REJOICE! FOR I HAVE DELIVERED YOU!" I freaked again and tried running to my bedroom next, hoping I might find some peace there. As I ran, however, this time, I began to feel a sense of joy flooding my being; it was unusual and a little scary—something I had never experienced before. Unable to hide in the bedroom, I was drawn slowly and cautiously back into the kitchen, where I heard the words again, "REJOICE FOR I HAVE DELIVERED YOU!" This time, these words brought me a sense of peace so deep I couldn't understand it . . . but I was still confused: *Who was this? Was it Jesus? Who else could it be but Him*, I thought. Again I heard the words, for the third time, "REJOICE FOR I HAVE DELIVERED YOU!" I sank to my knees, trembling and crying. At that point, I knew the living God was reaching out to me and rescuing me from hell.

A new, reverential fear I had never experienced before came over me as I sobbed on my knees. The entire experience had been unfolding for about twenty minutes when the song "Paradise Road" came to an end. I had been drawn into and immersed in the spiritual realm, and for the first time in my life, I was engulfed by a peace that truly surpassed my understanding. In that moment, it was difficult for me to comprehend what was happening, but the peace that washed over me was very real and indeed indescribable. Words cannot express the relief I felt in my heart, my mind, and my body. To that point, it felt like World War III or Armageddon had been taking place in my head.

Suddenly my mind was totally at peace, and the atmosphere was filled with a gentle calm. Everything was so light and quiet and serene. I then realized the war in my head had stopped! I looked outside and noticed the sky was vividly blue, and the trees were so green. Everything seemed so alive I kept thinking, *Is this what it feels like to be in Heaven? Is this really happening to me?* I marveled. *Is this what people refer to as being saved? Or being born-again?* I had used this term unknowingly several times in my life, "If ever I was born again (meaning if I could start afresh), I would never do the things I have done." I was instantly transported back to my early school years when, as a young boy, my two younger sisters and I attended a Catholic convent. Every day the whole convent would gather together in the assembly hall and recite Psalm 23: "The Lord is my Shepherd; I shall not want . . ." Verse 6 states, "Surely goodness and mercy shall follow me All the days of my life; And I will dwell in the house of the Lord Forever." For many years, while reciting this prayer, I wondered if, since I was such a rebel, I would actually dwell in the house of the Lord forever?

At the age of thirty-four, for the first time in my life, I experienced unexplainable tranquility like I had never known before. In that moment, I grasped this absolute reality: *Yes! I will dwell in the house of the Lord forever!* It brought pure joy to my soul. Hallelujah!

Inspired by this fresh, spiritual understanding, I immediately threw my drugs and alcohol away. If I had this . . . presence of God with me, I didn't need anything else. I had a shoebox filled with a substantial variety of pills and marijuana—I had just scored a stash of premium grass (weed) in Durban, on the lush east coast of South Africa. I pulled the shoebox out from under my bed and dumped it all in the garbage can. Next, I grabbed my daily two-liter jug of wine and poured it down the kitchen sink drain.

Goodbye Drugs, Gangs, and Guns

From that day in 1980 to this current day, I've never put another drop of alcohol to my lips. Neither have I smoked a joint nor even a cigarette, and I have never again lifted my hand to another man. I give all the praise, the glory, and the honor to the God of my salvation. Jesus truly delivered me and set me free. In an instant, I walked away from the world of drugs, gangs, and guns, leaving behind endless hatred, confusion, destruction, and death.

A few years later, under a deep, personal conviction, the Lord said to me, "Sell your guns." My guns were an idol to me and a link to that past world. Even though I had seventeen premium firearms, many of them collector's pieces, I didn't even think twice about it. I was instructed by God to give the money to a powerful ministry that was leading literally millions to the Lord in Africa. I obeyed and had never been happier.

From that glorious day in 1980, I have served the one and only true God. If the Son of God gives you freedom, no force in the universe can take it away. John's gospel makes this clear: "Therefore if the Son makes you free, you shall be free indeed" (John 8:36). To be free in Jesus is to be truly and completely free; nothing else can even remotely compare.

I didn't know it, but I had been searching for Jesus all my life. Reading through the annals of human history, we soon realize that throughout the ages, people have been searching for the same thing—someone to lead the way to God. We find the Answer in John's gospel: "Jesus said to him, *'I am the way,* the truth, and the life. No one comes to the Father except through Me'" (John 14:6— my emphasis).

Jesus is unequivocally the only "Way" to God! I am living proof of His love, kindness, and powerful deliverance!

Chapter Three

Not Ashamed

My mother's maiden name was Toweel, which I mention because the Toweels have become legendary within South African society as the greatest boxing dynasty in our nation's history. My cousin, Vic Toweel, was South Africa's first boxing world champion when there were only eight world titles in all weight classes and promotions.

In 1950, Vic beat the renowned Manuel Ortiz to become the world bantamweight champion in his fourteenth professional fight. Vic's brothers also won several national titles, and the boxing community gathered around them, so I grew up immersed in boxing, it becoming a major part of my life. I never made it big in the ring, but just training with my cousins gave me a tremendous fighting advantage. When it was clean competition, it was a very exciting time to follow and watch as relatives became champion boxers. The problem was that I had some skills and was willing to use them in not-so-clean competition.

Before My Encounter with Jesus

One night, before I gave my life to Jesus, one of my cousins had just won a South African national title. In my typically inebriated state in that era, I staggered up onto the ring apron to enthusiastically congratulate him on his victory. Of course, spectators were not allowed in or near the ring. Maybe because you could smell the alcohol from thirty feet away, I was immediately grabbed and punched by someone who probably assumed I was going to assault one of the boxers. Well, I punched back with a vengeance, and instantly a crazy fight broke out that ended up in a wild free-for-all at ringside.

The next day our local newspaper had me splashed across the front page: "HOOLIGANS AT RINGSIDE," read the Sunday headline news. The article featured two prominent pictures— one of me pounding an ex-boxer on the floor and another of me holding a policeman by the throat, ready to punch his lights out.

Why am I telling you all of this? Well, if I was not ashamed to live like a lunatic, drinking myself into a stupor at a boxing match and behaving like a hooligan for Satan at ringside, how can I possibly be ashamed of the glorious gospel of Christ now that I am a Christian?

Romans 1:16 says: "For I am not ashamed of the gospel of Christ, for it is the power of God to salvation for everyone who believes, for the Jew first and also for the Greek." No, I am not and never will be ashamed of the gospel of Christ! Especially since Jesus is not ashamed to call us brethren, as Hebrews 2:11b says: ". . . for which reason He is not ashamed to call them brethren."

Imagine for a moment, if you will, this holy, righteous God who loves us regardless of what we were but who also loves us for what we are becoming. We run from God, we cuss and carry on as if there is no God, but He reaches down to us and extends His love towards us; He washes us clean by the blood of Jesus. He forgives us for all of our sins. He is never ashamed to be called our God. What a beautiful Person He is.

Consider that Jesus became the ultimate disgrace for every one of us by hanging naked on a cross and dying in our place, but He did this because He is not ashamed to be called our God! You see, by accepting His sacrifice offered in our place, we are given eternal life through grace and faith, and this life is extended to all who will believe in Him.

The Start of My Ministry

From that amazing day in 1980, with God's presence in my life, things only turned upward. In 1981, my wife and I, being eager and enthusiastic Bible School students, wanted to do something for the Lord, so we visited our church's street outreach program. From the very first day, the Holy Spirit (and my wife, Dyllis) compelled me to join this ministry, but I was nervous because I was being sent back to the streets where I had once run amuck. I soon realized, however, it was my chance to make a difference where I had once only made trouble. My wife and I served faithfully, and after a few months, I was asked to preach. I was so nervous, but I knew God wanted me to do it. I took this opportunity very seriously and spent the whole week preparing a message on the trial and crucifixion of Christ—a topic that fascinated me (and still fascinates me to this day).

Eventually, the time came, and it was my turn to preach. I stepped forward to speak, but suddenly I was speechless! I froze with stage fright as the crowd stared at me, and I wondered, *What are they staring at?* I had the wonderful fifteen-point message in the back of my Bible on how Jesus was marred more than any man, how He was spat upon, blindfolded, slapped, and punched in the face. The wicked Roman soldiers jammed a crown of thorns on His head, then beat the crown into His head with a stick. He was tied up like a criminal, but He had never even sinned (detailed in Matthew 27:27-30).

I desperately tried to start this message I loved so much, but I could only stare, dumbfounded, not opening my Bible. Then I heard these words roaring out of my innermost being: "THE SAME GOD WHO ANOINTED JESUS OF NAZARETH TO PREACH THE GOSPEL ANOINTED PETER RAHME!" (This was in keeping with the verse from Acts 10:38). I was taken aback, as I could hear my own voice, but these were not my words.

In an instant rush, the power of God surged through me like lightning, changing my life forever, yet again. I preached a blazing Holy Spirit-fire-filled message for about fifteen minutes, then called for people to receive Christ. To my astonishment, about seventy people gave their lives to our wonderful Lord and Savior that day. I cried with joy, knowing how their lives were about to be changed and blessed, just like mine. My ministry had begun. Hallelujah!

That day–when I was obedient despite my nervousness–was the beginning of fourteen years of outreach ministry. We ministered weekly in the streets of Johannesburg and held mighty crusades in every major city in South Africa, as well as ministry in neighboring African countries and Europe. In that time, all of these outreaches brought in a harvest of hundreds of thousands of souls. All Glory to God!

[37] Then He said to His disciples, "The harvest is [indeed] plentiful, but the workers are few. [38] So pray to the Lord of the harvest to send out workers into His harvest." Matthew 9:37-38 (AMP)

God Can and Will Set Anyone Free

One day while preaching in the city center of Johannesburg, I was astonished to see several of the Jeppe gang members from my youth standing in the crowd listening to me share the gospel. I was floored when these men responded to the altar call and came forward to give their hearts to Jesus. How wonderful is our God? This is yet another example of our great God being willing and able to truly set anyone free. He had truly brought me full circle, blessing me beyond anything I could imagine in seeing these men also receive His love and forgiveness. Romans 5:20-21 states: "[20] But where sin abounded, grace abounded much more, [21] so that as sin reigned in death, even so grace might reign through righteousness to eternal life through Jesus Christ our Lord." Hallelujah!

Visual Aids

When I started preaching in the open-air ministry our church had founded, the Lord revealed how powerful visual aids are. He impressed upon me that the cross, the crown of thorns, and the three nails, were strong visual aids I could use to demonstrate the love of Christ. Throughout the world, everyone knows Jesus was crucified on a cross, but when they saw the huge cross, the whip with bone and metal shards, and the sharp crown of thorns, Jesus' sacrifice became very real. The cross also always signifies Jesus Christ and how He was crucified to redeem people, so it was an excellent visual tool to draw people from afar.

I once heard a statistic that people retain seventy percent of a visual message. I know firsthand it worked wonders in our outreaches.

The Way, the Truth, and the Life

One particular day while preaching in the streets of Johannesburg, I explained the truth about Jesus being the only way to reach God the Father. Jesus, speaking to Thomas, said, "I am the way, the truth, and the life. No one comes to the Father except through Me" (John 14:6). I preached about Jesus being the only way, explaining to the crowd before me that "the way" is like a road or a freeway, leading us to a specific destination. What happened next cannot be accurately articulated—I am unable to explain it in the natural, but for about five seconds, my eyes were opened to the spiritual realm, and I saw the road I was standing on receding into the distance, then going up all the way to Heaven. This vision of "the way" disappeared as suddenly as it had appeared. From that moment in time, I have known without any doubt Jesus is and will always be the Way throughout eternity.

I believe the Lord revealed to me, in a very personal manner, the identity of the Lord Jesus Christ, who truly is the only way to reach God the Father. The following truths about Jesus entirely changed me when I began delving into scripture.

Jesus is divine Truth, and He is the Life-giver to all people. Another verse of scripture I really love is found in Ephesians: "If indeed you have heard Him and have been taught by Him, as **the truth is in Jesus** . . ." (Ephesians 4:21—my emphasis). Another scripture that reveals Jesus as being divine truth is found in John's gospel: "For the law was given through Moses, but grace and truth came through Jesus Christ" (John 1:17).

Jesus is Our Peace

The prophet Isaiah prophesied about Israel's Messiah, who would ultimately bring peace to the entire Earth:

> For unto us a Child is born, Unto us a Son is given; And the government will be upon His shoulder. And His name will be called Wonderful, Counselor, Mighty God, Everlasting Father, Prince of Peace. Isaiah 9:6

As I said before, I am living proof of Jesus being our complete Peace.

Jesus is Different Because He Never Committed a Sin

What sets Jesus apart from any other prophet or man who has lived? To understand why Jesus is different, the Bible tells us the angel Gabriel appeared to Mary and said to her, "And behold, you will conceive in your womb and bring forth a Son, and shall call His name Jesus" (Luke 1:31). He also said to her, "The Holy Spirit will come upon you, and the power of the Highest will overshadow you; therefore, also, that Holy One who is to be born will be called the Son of God" (Luke 1:35).

This is no fairy tale. It is very real, and Jesus was born of a virgin for a very specific reason. Thousands of people have tried to dispute the truths found in the Bible, but once they honestly study it, they find the truth *is* in Jesus.

When Jesus was born of the Holy Spirit and a virgin, He did not inherit *man's* sinful nature. Even though Eve also sinned, Adam was responsible for the decision, and his blood was corrupted. Jesus was born without this corrupted, sinful *nature*. Yet, He was tested and tempted more than any person who ever walked the Earth because He carried such a great responsibility, and Satan wanted to see Him fail. Yes, Jesus could definitely have failed; otherwise, His life and sacrifice would not have been legitimate. What sets Jesus apart from any other prophet or alleged prophet or "holy man" is that Jesus lived and died without committing any sin:

For we do not have a High Priest who is unable to sympathize and understand our weaknesses and temptations, but One who has been tempted [knowing exactly how it feels to be human] in every respect as we are, yet without [committing any] sin. Hebrews 4:15 (AMP)

Praise the Lord that we have literally God Himself, Who came down in the flesh and walked with us, showing us the way. This revelation changed my life as a young believer. I had dabbled in all sorts of weird stuff trying to find the truth, so when I found Jesus and realized He was unlike any of the other imitations, I *knew* I had found the one and only Truth!

John 8:31-36:

[31] Then Jesus said to those Jews who believed Him, "If you abide in My word, you are My disciples indeed. [32] And you shall know the truth, and the truth shall make you free."

[33] They answered Him, "We are Abraham's descendants, and have never been in bondage to anyone. How *can* You say, 'You will be made free'?"

[34] Jesus answered them, "Most assuredly, I say to you, whoever commits sin is a slave of sin. [35] And a slave does not abide in the house forever, *but* a son abides forever. [36] Therefore if the Son makes you free, you shall be free indeed.

Chapter Four

There is Only One Savior of Mankind

It amazes me that people look for salvation in all the wrong places, despite scripture being very clear about there being only one form of salvation available to us. I know there is a trend these days to be politically correct and claim there are many ways to Heaven to avoid offending anyone—but that is simply *not* the truth. Why would you lie to people just to make them feel better? No, I want everyone to be truly set free!

All three scriptures below point to Jesus alone being the Savior of the world.

Salvation in No One Else

"There is salvation in no one else! For there is no other name under heaven given to mankind by whom we must be saved!" Acts 4:12 (CJB)

There Is Only One Mediator between God and Men

There is only one mediator between God and men! You don't need anyone to offer your prayers to God or tell you what or how to pray—God desires a personal, one-on-one relationship with you. Never doubt that. "For there is one God and one Mediator between God and men, the Man Christ Jesus . . ." (1 Timothy 2:5).

Salvation in No Other Name

The apostle Peter made it very clear we must build our lives on Jesus, who is the chief Cornerstone of God's redemption plan for humanity:

> [10] Let it be known to you all, and to all the people of Israel, that by the name of Jesus Christ of Nazareth, whom you crucified, whom God raised from the dead, by Him this man stands here before you whole. [11] This is the 'stone which was rejected by you builders, which has become the chief cornerstone.' [12] Nor is there salvation in any other, for there is no other name under heaven given among men by which we must be saved. Acts 4:10-12

Considering these scriptures, it seems absurd to look for another savior when the Bible, the most reliable document in antiquity, which is God's holy Word, is so emphatic concerning this matter.

There are currently over two billion people who believe Jesus is the only Savior of the world. Yes, many would try to dispute the Bible as the Word of God and even the life, death, and resurrection of Jesus. We can describe how the Bible is the most authentic and consistent record in antiquity *by far*, using the legal-historical method—but that *still* won't convince some people. The truth is your heart convicts you of the truth. Only by reaching a point where you are genuinely and desperately seeking the truth will you stand at the crossroad where you are ready to receive.

I can assure you from a personal, living testimony Jesus truly *is* the Son of God, the Savior of the world. He set me free and changed my life completely, and *you, too*, can experience His love, peace, joy, and tranquility for the rest of your days—if you would *only believe* and receive.

We are all meant to share in the eternal life God offers us through His Son, Jesus, which is clearly referenced in the passage below:

> [16] For God so loved the world that He gave His only begotten Son, that whoever believes in Him should not perish but have everlasting life. [17] For God did not send His Son into the world to condemn the world, but that the world through Him might be saved. John 3:16-17

I urge you to pray out loud the prayer printed in Chapter Four—all you have to do is read the prayer, pray it from your heart, believe it, and I promise you will receive salvation! Truly, Jesus will set you free too.

If you have already prayed that prayer and have put your trust in Him, it is important you act on what you believe by telling others of your Lord's life-changing and amazing grace. I used to live each day focused exclusively on what I could get out of life for myself. All my energy was focused on my own selfishness, my own greed, and my own desires. I thought I was operating in love because I showed love to my family and my friends—but my love was conditional. I operated out of my own motives and focused solely on what I could get out of it.

Rumor has it that Frank Sinatra, the multi-millionaire who popularized the song, (I Did It) "My Way," hoping for salvation, once asked Pope John Paul II to hear his confession. Apparently, the pope declined, despite Mr. Sinatra's promise to give the pope half of his wealth if the pope could acquit him of his sins. Sadly, even for Frank Sinatra, this was never going to happen. There is not a human being on Earth who can save us.

We know this because the Bible says in Romans 3:23: "For all have sinned and fall short of the glory of God." We are all in the same boat. To reiterate, Jesus of Nazareth was not born of a human father—His blood was not contaminated by sin, as is our blood, conceived by men. To maintain the purity of His Son being born in a human form, God the Father used a virgin, touched by the Holy Spirit, to bring His Son into the world to save the world. This is how the apostle Paul puts it:

> Here is how it works: it was through one individual (Adam) that sin entered the world, and through sin, death; and in this way death passed through to the whole human race, inasmuch as everyone sinned. Romans 5:12 (CJB—my addition in parentheses).

It's important to recognize you are a spirit, you live in a body, and you have a soul, as expressed in scripture: "Now may the God of peace Himself sanctify you completely; and may your whole spirit, soul, and body be preserved blameless at the coming of our Lord Jesus Christ" (1 Thessalonians 5:23).

The Human Condition

The fact that we are spirits living in bodies makes sense when considering how we treat each other. Most people try to live by their convictions: we take time to please others, to be courteous, loving, and kind. You don't need a wise old man to tell you how vital these things are to being human— they are self-evident. So where do these actions of innate decency come from if we are only a body and a brain? If we are not eternal spirits inhabiting physical bodies, what does it matter if we live selfish, greedy lives driven by primal animal instincts? If we have no spirit, and human life literally ends when we suffer physical death, what prompts us to behave any less savagely than animals? Some people around the world do indeed behave like brute beasts, but the vast majority of us have a good amount of care for our fellow man and woman.

For me, the ultimate proof lies in the fact that once you have personally encountered the living God, the overall change in a person is easily identifiable. A person who has genuinely been born-again changes completely. They have a natural love for people and a "brightness" and lightness that is very visible. Their *heart* changes. Your heart can change too.

To have such an encounter, you must reach out to God in faith, believing He exists. It would be foolish to ask someone to help you if you don't believe they even exist, right? But you can't see God! Why not? Well, because He is holy and all-powerful. In our sinful state, we would be instantly evaporated if we were to be placed in God's presence. Still, God offers us grace, which is taken hold of by faith. The following scripture puts this into better perspective: "For by grace you have been saved through faith, and that not of yourselves; it is the gift of God" (Ephesians 2:8).

You have been created beautifully, perfectly, and magnificently by the hand of God, whether you believe it or not. These are not words to please you but to awaken you. I tell you this to show you your life is more than work, food, drink, and sleep—we are not meant to live aimlessly, day by day. American author and motivational speaker Zig Ziglar coined this phrase, "If you aim at nothing, you will hit it every time." Unfortunately, this is how we tend to live—embracing the careless attitude that "whatever will be will be."Yet the Bible assures us we are lovingly created by God. King David says in the Book of Psalms: "I will praise You, for I am fearfully and wonderfully made; Marvelous are Your works, And that my soul knows very well." Psalm 139:14. If this is true, surely God created us with a purpose in mind? If we are created with a purpose, then adopting a careless attitude to life must be contrary to God's plan for us?

There is not a person on Earth who was created by mistake. On the contrary, Jesus assured us of God's devotion to our well-being, saying, "But the very hairs of your head are all numbered" (Matthew 10:30). God, speaking to the Old Testament prophet, Jeremiah, explains to him in intricate detail how involved in our lives He truly is, from birth to death: "Before I formed you in the womb I knew you; Before you were born I sanctified you; I ordained you a prophet to the nations" (Jeremiah 1:5).

There isn't a person on this planet who God does not know down to the smallest detail. God knows everything about you. He knows all your hurts, pains, and suffering—He knows your ups and downs. Only God the Father, His wonderful Son, and His marvelous Spirit truly know you. You are unique. There are no duplicates on Earth, no two people are identical, and the same goes for animals and trees. God, in His wisdom, splendor, and beauty, chose not to make two people alike. He made you unique, so He can love you with all your flaws, mistakes, and hopelessness. When He turns your shortcomings to His glory, all He asks in return is that you love Him and give Him the honor and praise for first loving you in your worst state; so that He can now love you in your best state! Hallelujah!

I know the Father's love because Jesus saved me from death and destruction. He also saved billions of others, who have all been snatched out of Satan's clutches—the one who came to steal, to kill, and to destroy (paraphrase of John 10:10). Jesus ends this verse of scripture by saying, ". . . I have come that they may have life, and that they may have it more abundantly." Or you can say *superabundantly*.

Don't Reject This Gift

Imagine rejecting such a wonderful gift? The very Son of God taking our punishment and death sentence upon Himself so we wouldn't have to? That's pure love. What happens, however, if a person rejects such a sacrificial gift? The Bible refers to "the second death[2]" as separation from God the Father and His Son for all eternity. Take a moment to consider what is presented in the Bible and what God expects of us. If God presents

His Son as humanity's only Savior, then surely He has to give us detailed information about how Jesus qualifies as our Savior? If Jesus is to be our Savior, He has to be God, who has come down to Earth in the flesh. He has to be pure, holy, and sinless if He was sent to save us. Otherwise, He would be just like us and would be subject to the same messy lives we lead. Don't take my word—rather, let me share some biblical truths with you, and you can decide for yourself if Jesus qualifies to be your Savior. As you read the scriptures below, you will almost certainly feel convicted and desire to repent of your sins, so you can be washed clean by Jesus Christ through God's Word.

If God isn't who He says He is, then He would never have given us the Bible, which was written over a period of 4,000 years through various God-appointed and God-inspired people.

Adam Committed High Treason

Genesis 2:16-17 says: "[16] And the Lord God commanded the man, saying, 'Of every tree of the garden you may freely eat; [17] but of the tree of the knowledge of good and evil you shall not eat, for in the day that you eat of it you shall surely die.'"

As a note here, the original Hebrew text[3] uses an idiomatic construction translated directly as "in dying, you shall die." In more straightforward English, the words used for "surely" and "die" are the same Hebrew word—*mût*—but are used together as an idiom to say "in dying you will die." This means Adam experienced two deaths. Even though he sinned when he ate the fruit of this tree, he didn't drop dead instantly—he lived on to be 930 years old in his physical body (Genesis 5:5). Although Adam did not immediately succumb to physical death, he died spiritually that same day, and was banished from the garden. He was separated from God and God's life-giving power.

Bear in mind the Bible is always consistent. If Adam suffered two deaths, then there would have to be two births for God's redemption plan to be effective. We are thus born once from our mother and born-again of the Holy Spirit, as we see in John's gospel:

> [3] Jesus answered and said to him, 'Most assuredly, I say to you, unless one is born again, he cannot see the kingdom of God.'

> [4] Nicodemus said to Him, 'How can a man be born when he is old? Can he enter a second time into his mother's womb and be born?'

> [5] Jesus answered, 'Most assuredly, I say to you, unless one is born of water and the Spirit, he cannot enter the kingdom of God. [6] That which is born of the flesh is flesh, and that which is born of the Spirit is spirit. [7] Do not marvel that I said to you, 'You must be born again." John 3:3-7

Jesus refers to our physical birth through water, after which we must choose to be born of the Spirit if we wish to enter God's eternal Kingdom.

Back to the Garden

To understand this more clearly, consider that after Adam and Eve had disobeyed God's one rule, He immediately set into motion a plan to redeem His people:

> [14] So the Lord God said to the serpent: 'Because you have done this, You are cursed more than all cattle, And more than every beast of the field; On your belly you shall go, And you shall eat dust All the days of your life. [15] And I will put enmity Between you and the woman, And between your seed and "her Seed"; He shall bruise your head, And you shall bruise His heel.' Genesis 3:14-15

This passage from the Book of Genesis gives us great insight into a verse from Paul's letter to the Galatians: "But when the appointed time arrived, God sent forth his Son. He was born from a woman . . ." (Partial rendition of Galatians 4:4—CJB).

Only one Person throughout the ages was born through the seed of a woman, with no man involved in conception. Before Jesus, no one had even considered the concept. The rest of humanity was born through the (corrupted) seed of a man—only Jesus was born through the seed of a woman, touched by the Holy Spirit; He was born of a virgin named Mary.

In the Book of Isaiah, we are given a prophecy concerning the birth of Christ, the Messiah: "Therefore the Lord Himself will give you a sign: Behold, the virgin shall conceive and bear a Son, and shall call His name Immanuel" (Isaiah 7:14). The name "Immanuel" literally means, "God-With-Us."

Yet another prophecy concerning the birth of the Messiah is again written in the Book of Isaiah: "For unto us a Child is born, Unto us a Son is given; And the government will be upon His shoulder. And His name will be called Wonderful, Counselor, Mighty God, Everlasting Father, Prince of Peace" (Isaiah 9:6).

The New Testament also reflects the divinity of Jesus Christ, confirming Isaiah 7:14: "'Behold, the virgin shall be with child, and bear a Son, and they shall call His name Immanuel,' which is translated, 'God with us'" (Matthew 1:23).

According to the Biblical timeline, 4,000 years had passed before Jesus was introduced to the Earth in His physical form. He was born in Bethlehem, a tiny city just a fraction bigger than four square miles. God announced His Son's arrival by setting a bright star in the heavens, one of the celestial signs causing wise men to travel from the far east to see the newborn baby, the King of kings. The mostly-symbolic king in Israel named Herod heard about the Child, trying to protect his dynasty, and in a parallel to Pharaoh trying to kill Moses, ordered the execution of all newborn male children in Israel.

God protected Jesus, of course, and when He came of age, He announced His arrival in the synagogue as "God's anointed One." The crowd of self-seeking religious leaders who witnessed this event went berserk, wanting to throw Jesus off a cliff (detailed in Luke 4). Many other similar incidents exist; men despised and rejected Jesus, but they could not prevent the Son of God from fulfilling the work set out for Him by His Father. The Bible tells us *why* Jesus was sent to Earth: ". . . For this purpose the Son of God was manifested, that He might destroy the works of the devil" (1 John 3:8b).

When Jesus fasted in the wilderness for forty days and nights, the devil tried the same tactic he had used against Adam and Eve, fulfilling the prophecy God made all the way back in Genesis regarding enmity between the Seed of the woman and the seed of the serpent: "And the devil said to Him, 'If You are the Son of God, command this stone to become bread'" (Luke 4:3). The devil will always test you when you are experiencing low points in your life. Thankfully, knowing scripture enables us to overcome these tests. "4 But Jesus answered him, saying, 'It is written, "Man shall not live by bread alone, but by every word of God."'" The devil brought more temptations to Jesus during that time of testing. Although the temptations were very real, Jesus trounced the devil every step of the way using the Word of God.

We are given excellent advice to this effect in James 4:7, which says, "Therefore submit to

God. Resist the devil and he will flee from you." Once you have accepted Jesus as your Lord and Savior, you immediately receive His authority and power of attorney to resist the devil. By using the mighty name of Jesus against the devil and knowing and speaking God's Word to the devil, he has no option but to flee as he did from Jesus. Hallelujah!

Jesus Was Sent by God the Father

So we have established that Jesus was born of a virgin, a miracle by earthly standards. This puts Jesus into a category of His own:

- He never committed a sin (Hebrews 4:15).
- He lived a spotless life so He could be a sacrifice from God for all of humanity (1 Peter 1:19).
- John the Baptist saw Jesus and said, "Behold! The Lamb of God who takes away the sin of the world!" (John 1:29).
- Jesus was born to be a sacrificial Lamb of God (Revelation 5:12).
- He was put on a wooden cross and nailed to it for each and every one of us (Colossians 2:14).
- He became a curse for us (Galatians 3:13).
- He became sin for us (2 Corinthians 5:21).
- There is only one Savior of mankind: "There is salvation in no one else! For there is no other name under heaven given to mankind by whom we must be saved!" (Acts 4:12—CJB).

You Can Make Jesus Your Lord Today

I shared my testimony and all these truths about Jesus, hoping you now also believe Jesus is the only Savior of Mankind. If you were the only person on Earth, God the Father would still have sent His only begotten Son and raised Him from the dead to save you and stop the war raging for your soul. You, too, can experience the peace, love, and joy I have, no matter what you've done.

I believe the Holy Spirit has touched your heart with my true story, as I am a witness that Jesus can and will instantly do it for you too! You are not reading this book by accident. Please pray the following prayer. If you believe it in your heart, just pray it out loud, and you *will* be saved:

> Lord God, I come to you in the wonderful name of Your holy Son, Jesus. I am sorry for my sins of rebelling against your good and true Way. I repent—promising to turn away from my sins, and I ask Your forgiveness for all my wrongdoing. Your Word says, 'whoever calls on the name of the Lord shall be saved.' I confess with my mouth this day before Heaven and Earth that I make Jesus my Lord and believe in my heart that God has raised Him from the dead so I can be raised to new life with the same power of Your Holy Spirit.
>
> Lord, Your Word says, "For with the heart one believes unto righteousness, and with the mouth confession is made unto salvation," so I am submitting to You in this belief and

confession of Jesus, fully believing I am now saved.

I believe from this moment forward I am washed in the purifying blood of Jesus, I am saved from my formerly wicked ways, and I am now born of your Spirit.

Thank you, my heavenly Dad, for saving and forgiving me in Jesus' wonderful name. Amen! (Romans 10:9-10, 13).

Praise God! What a day this is! If you prayed this prayer and meant it, you have just been born of the Holy Spirit, adopted into God's eternal family. You are now a royal child of the Most High God, and you will live forever with God in eternal love, joy, and peace! Hallelujah! Welcome to the family of God. You have just inherited eternal life. Your spirit is now alive to God. You are washed clean and made brand new!

But wait . . . there's more!

Since you have just been born again, there is no reason to not be filled with the Holy Spirit too! The sweet Holy Spirit of God will empower you to walk your daily life close to God. He is a Person, and He is right there with you, ready to fill you with His joy and power. Please keep reading so you have a thorough understanding of who the Holy Spirit is and what baptism into the Holy Spirit is. I guarantee you want this gift.

Chapter Five

The Holy Spirit

The subject of the infilling of the Holy Spirit with power is so important, and more so than ever in our current times, that I wanted to add a chapter on this topic in the revised edition of this book. As I have mentioned, there is a distinct difference between being saved by Jesus (born-again) and being baptized into the Holy Spirit. Yes, you can be saved without the baptism of the Holy Spirit, but you won't be nearly as effective as you will be with the power of the Holy Spirit. Yes, you have the Spirit of Christ living within you when you are saved, but His indwelling presence is different to His baptism with fire (Matthew 3:11).

All the disciples believed in Jesus being the Messiah (Hebrew) or Christ (Greek), but the day of Pentecost was a totally different occurrence that went beyond salvation—never confuse the two. The Spirit baptizes one into the body of Christ, but the Lord Jesus Christ baptizes one into the Spirit of God.

Jesus Was Born of the Holy Spirit

To start, below are a few scriptures that show the relationship between Jesus and the Holy Spirit:

"She (Mary) was found with child of the Holy Spirit" (Matthew 1:18—my addition in parentheses).

"Joseph, son of David, do not be afraid to take to you Mary your wife, for that which is conceived in her *is of the Holy Spirit*" (Matthew 1:20—my emphasis).

Jesus Was Filled with and Led by the Holy Spirit

"Then Jesus, being *filled with* the Holy Spirit, returned from the Jordan and was *led by* the Spirit into the wilderness" (Luke 4:1—my emphasis).

Note that it was after this experience of the infilling of the Holy Spirit that Jesus returned with power to begin His ministry. Jesus did not do one miracle before He was filled with the Holy Spirit.

Jesus Baptizes Us with the Holy Spirit

Referring to Jesus, John the Baptist said:

It's true that I am immersing you in water so that you might turn from sin to God; but the one coming after me is more powerful than I—I'm not worthy even to carry his sandals—and he will immerse you in the *Ruach HaKodesh* (the Holy Spirit) and in fire. (Matthew 3:11, CJB— my addition in parentheses).

Jesus Casts Out Demons by the Spirit

The scripture that should be paid attention to most closely by anyone saying the gift of tongues is of the devil is Matthew 12:28. Remember, speaking in other tongues (languages) by divine utterance is the evidence of the infilling of the Holy Spirit: "But if I cast out demons by the Spirit of God, surely the kingdom of God has come upon you" (Matthew 12:28).

Saying the baptism into the Holy Spirit with the evidence of speaking in other tongues is not of God, or worse, demonic, is akin to blaspheming the Holy Spirit.

The Father Will Give You the Holy Spirit

The amazing news is that Jesus made it clear all who ask will receive the Holy Spirit from the Father. Jesus was saying you can trust God will not give you a snake when you ask Him for a fish: "If you then, being evil, know how to give good gifts to your children, how much more will your heavenly Father give the Holy Spirit to those who ask Him!" (Luke 11:13).

All Were Baptized into the Holy Spirit

Let's dive deeper into what it means to be baptized into the Spirit of God. We find the answer in the book of Acts:

> ¹ When the Day of Pentecost had fully come, they were all with one accord in one place. ² And suddenly there came a sound from heaven, as of a rushing mighty wind, and it filled the whole house where they were sitting. ³ Then there appeared to them divided tongues, as of fire, and one sat upon each of them. ⁴ And they were all filled with the Holy Spirit and began to speak with other tongues, as the Spirit gave them utterance. Acts 2:1-4

The day of Pentecost is known on the Jewish calendar as *Shavuoth*—originally a harvest festival, which now also commemorates the giving of the Law (the Torah). *Shavuoth* is also called Pentecost or Feast of Weeks. The day of Pentecost happened on precisely the fiftieth day (seven weeks) after the end of the Passover feast and the resurrection of Messiah Christ.

Take note, it was the *Holy Spirit* who enabled them to speak with other tongues, as He, the Spirit, gave them the words to say. For this reason, being baptized into the Holy Spirit and speaking with other tongues as the Holy Spirit gives you the words is vital in building yourself up daily, so you will be bold in your witnessing for Christ.

Many in the body of Christ talk about the Holy Spirit but do not give Him the time necessary to know Him and build a close and deep relationship with Him. Throughout the life of Christ, the Spirit of God was the one who led Jesus, who operated in and through Him, and was the most important Person in Jesus' life, along with the Father.

Jesus was born of the Holy Spirit and did all His miracles through the Holy Spirit. The scriptures below reveal specific points that led to Jesus' success. Let's go through them so you are able to understand the life and work of the Spirit in Jesus' life. Besides being born-again, there is nothing more vital than being baptized into the Holy Spirit. To lead a Spirit-led life, you must keep praying in the Spirit, which enables you to build yourself up in the Holy Spirit.

This is why the apostle Paul encouraged Timothy to practice the gifts he was given when he wrote, "Therefore I remind you to stir up the gift of God which is in you through the laying on of my hands" (2 Timothy 1:6). In his letter to the Ephesian church, Paul also advised the congregation, "but be filled with the Spirit" (Ephesians 5:18b).

You Have Been Born-Again by the Spirit of God

Speaking to Nicodemus, "Jesus answered, 'Most assuredly, I say to you, unless one is born of water and the Spirit, he cannot enter the kingdom of

God. [6] That which is born of the flesh is flesh, and that which is born of the Spirit is spirit'" (John 3:5-6).

Jesus Promises Us Power from the Holy Spirit

In Acts 1:8 Jesus gives us a compelling and mighty promise: "You shall receive power when the Holy Spirit has come upon you; and you shall be witnesses to Me in Jerusalem, and in all Judea and Samaria, and to the end of the earth."

Once you receive the infilling of the Spirit, this power is greater than any other power this world can offer you. It is God Himself, the Holy Spirit, the third Person of the Trinity, who comes to dwell in you and take up permanent residence within you while you walk this Earth. He was present when God created this entire material universe (Genesis 1:2), and He now lives within *you!*

Jesus specifically promised us the help of the Holy Spirit:

> [16] And I will pray the Father, and He will give you another Helper, that He may abide with you forever—[17] the Spirit of truth, whom the world cannot receive, because it neither sees Him nor knows Him; but you know Him, for He dwells with you and will be in you. John 14:16-17.

This means that being baptized into the Holy Spirit enables you to be an effective witness for Christ.

This miracle-working power energizes every believer who chooses to trust God above all else, so we can be led, guided, governed, and controlled by the Holy Spirit. Having received this powerful Helper, I have made it my duty to lead people to the Lord on a near-daily basis, witnessing to all who are sent my way. Just as the apostle Paul explained to King Agrippa, "Therefore, having obtained help from God, to this day I stand, witnessing both to small and great, saying no other things than those which the prophets and Moses said would come" (Acts 26:22).

Jesus Heals All by the Holy Spirit

In Luke 4:18-19 Jesus repeats Isaiah's prophecy, demonstrating that the Spirit of the Lord was upon Jesus for this very purpose—to anoint Him for ministry:

> [18] The Spirit of the Lord *is* upon Me,
> Because He has anointed Me
> To preach the gospel to *the* poor;
> He has sent Me to heal the brokenhearted,
> To proclaim liberty to *the* captives
> And recovery of sight to *the* blind,
> *To* set at liberty those who are oppressed;
> [19] To proclaim the acceptable year of the Lord.

Similarly, Acts 10:38 reiterates, "How God anointed Jesus of Nazareth with the Holy Spirit and with power, who went about doing good and *healing all* who were oppressed by the devil, for God was with Him."

You Have Been Sealed by the Holy Spirit

Did you know the Holy Spirit is your seal—meaning your guarantee of eternal life? Ephesians 4:30 says, "And do not grieve the Holy Spirit of God, by whom you were sealed for the day of redemption." Every believer has been sealed with the Holy Spirit to take them safely to the other side. In Heaven, there is no time, sin, sickness, disease, pain, worry, or tragedy—the last enemy to be put under our feet is death itself: "The last enemy that will be destroyed is death" (1 Corinthians 15:26).

Now, as we move on, remember that Jesus is the *only One* who saves and baptizes into the Holy Spirit. Prior to your birth, God predestined and called you to walk in righteousness and be an imitator of Jesus Christ. God's plan is well orchestrated: the Holy Spirit is holy—He is the absolute embodiment of holiness—and He, therefore, enables *us* to be holy, which is crucial to our consistent progression of faith.

He is also called the Spirit of promise in numerous Bible verses, of which Ephesians 1:13 is one example: "In Him you also *trusted,* after you heard the word of truth, the gospel of your salvation; in whom also, having believed, you were sealed with the Holy Spirit of promise." This means He sets us apart from the world for God, and we are marked as belonging to Him, as His very own special possession.

Speaking in Tongues

Now let's fully dive into the controversial topic of tongues. Speaking in tongues (or praying in the Spirit, as I prefer to call it) is the initial sign of being filled with the Holy Spirit for Jews and Gentiles alike. This is described in Mark 16:17: "And these signs will follow those who believe: In My name they will cast out demons; they will speak with new tongues."Tongues were given to the body of Christ for spiritual edification: "He who speaks in a tongue edifies himself, but he who prophesies edifies the church" (1 Corinthians 14:4). In this way, tongues remind us of the Spirit's indwelling presence and cause His power to flow through us: "For he who speaks in a tongue does not speak to men but to God, for no one understands him; however, in the spirit he speaks mysteries" (1 Corinthians 14:2).

This point is reiterated in 1 Corinthians 14:14, which tells us, "For if I pray in a tongue, my spirit prays, but my understanding is unfruitful." Indeed, tongues enable believers to stay in line with God's perfect will, allowing the Spirit to intercede on our behalf rather than leaning on our own understanding:

> [26] Likewise the Spirit also helps in our weaknesses. For we do not know what we should pray for as we ought, but the Spirit Himself makes intercession for us with groanings which cannot be uttered. [27] Now He who searches the hearts knows what the mind of the Spirit *is,* because He makes

intercession for the saints according to *the will of* God. Romans 8:26-27

Praying in tongues also stimulates our faith: "But you, beloved, build yourselves up on [the foundation of] your most holy faith [continually progress, rise like an edifice higher and higher], pray in the Holy Spirit" (Jude 1:20, AMP).

Your Spirit Prays When Speaking in Tongues

Praying in tongues is a great blessing, as your spirit talks directly to the Father through the Holy Spirit: "[14] For if I pray in a tongue, my spirit prays, but my understanding is unfruitful. [15] What is *the conclusion* then? I will pray with the spirit, and I will also pray with the understanding. I will sing with the spirit, and I will also sing with the understanding" (1 Corinthians 14:14-15). I encourage you to read the entire fourteenth chapter of 1 Corinthians for a more profound knowledge of the Holy Spirit.

Shortly before His death on the cross, Jesus encouraged His disciples, promising His Father would send them another Helper:

[15] If you love Me, keep My commandments. [16] And I will pray the Father, and He will give you another Helper, that He may abide with you forever—[17] the Spirit of truth, whom the world cannot receive, because it neither sees Him nor knows Him; but you know Him, for He dwells with you and will be in you. [18] I will not leave you orphans; I will come to you. John 14:15-18

I have come to the conclusion that without the Holy Spirit leading me daily, I cannot be very successful, nor am I living up to the standard to which Jesus has called me. If we walk in godly character and integrity, as we should, we will see the most extraordinary miracles, signs, and wonders this world has ever seen. We are heirs of God and joint heirs with Christ (Romans 8:17), so we can overcome any and every obstacle thrown at us if we only allow the Holy Spirit full access in and through our lives. He is marvelous, gentle, and kind—and He waits for us daily to ask Him to lead us into all wisdom and truth.

Let's pray and ask our Father to fill you with His precious Holy Spirit:

> Father, I want to know and be baptized into and filled with Your Holy Spirit to overflowing. I want to be led by Him, guided by Him, and controlled by Him for the rest of my life. Holy Spirit, I love You! I want to be baptized with your powerful fire! You are the Spirit of Christ—of my Lord Jesus. Fill me now so your power enables me to do our Father's will. I pray this in Jesus' precious name. Amen.

Hallelujah! You should feel the power of God in you right now! Speak in faith, and the Holy Spirit will give you the words to say. Keep practicing and speaking your heavenly language!

To learn more about your new gift and the power you received, read Acts 2:1-4 and Romans 8:14. You now have the most astounding and powerful Treasure within you! The Holy Spirit is with you 24/7, so learn to rely on Him, hear His voice, and be sensitive to His leading. He only wants the very best for you.

Praise God! This is a big day for you! The biggest day of your life. You are born again and filled with God's Holy Spirit. You can do *anything* He calls you to, and believe me, He has *big* plans for you! I pray our Lord and Savior heals you in every area and protects you as you serve Him and tell others of His wonderful love and grace.

What are the next steps? Well, to grow in the knowledge of your Savior, Jesus Christ, so you can emulate Him and totally fulfill the very unique and specific purpose God has for you. If you think you don't have the courage to fulfill God's purpose for your life, part of that being to share God's good news with others, you don't need courage . . . you just need the *boldness* that came with your infilling of the Holy Spirit!

Now, perhaps you are someone who once accepted Jesus as Lord, but you feel like you've grown cold. You don't have that fire any longer. You have been hurt, and your once bright future in God is lost. The next chapter carries extremely good news for you! God always has a fresh start and a plan to restore *everything* you've lost!

Keep reading, and I'll tell you how I went from being timid as a mouse to being bold as a lion!

Chapter Six

Stand Bold. Stand Strong

Mark's gospel presents a clear picture of why we should boldly proclaim our affiliation to Jesus: "For whoever is ashamed of Me and My words in this adulterous and sinful generation, of him the Son of Man also will be ashamed when He comes in the glory of His Father with the holy angels" (Mark 8:38).

God wants His children to be just like Jesus—so fired up, so charged up with the Holy Spirit we will literally change and charge the atmosphere around us with God's goodness and power. Then, wherever we go, cancerous growths will fall off people, and all sickness and demons will leave—like the demons who screamed and fled when they saw Jesus. God wants His people to speak the Word as Peter and John did at the Gate called Beautiful so the lame, the maimed, and the crippled will jump up and start skipping and dancing like young calves in the field (Acts 3:1-11).

God wants us to be bold and courageous, not afraid nor dismayed, for He is with us always! He wants His people to be like Caleb, who, at eighty-five years old, said, "Let us go up at once and take possession (of the Promised Land), for we are well able to overcome it" (Numbers 13:30—my addition in parentheses). We are ready, willing, and have more than enough power available to take our world back from the devil. God wants everyone to know about His love, compassion, and grace available to all humankind.

God wants us to stand firm—as if we were embedded in concrete—rooted and grounded in His Word, His name, and His love. Unshakeable, unmovable, rooted, and grounded in Christ who is the Captain of our salvation. Hallelujah!

God wants us to look the devil in the eye and say, "Devil, it is written, and there is nothing you or your forces can do to stop the move of God. Nor can you stop His people from reigning victorious on the Earth. Bow your knee to the King of kings and the Lord of lords!" And the devil will obey you because he has no choice (Luke 10:19). You are a royal dignitary of Heaven carrying the full force of Heaven's angelic military might behind you.

It's All about Jesus

Friend, the secret to boldness is knowing that it is all about Jesus. We must simply be followers and imitators of Him, walking in His footsteps and speaking His Word. We must say what He said and do what He did. He asks for nothing more and nothing less. It is easy once you learn how, so how about it?

Let's go into the highways and the byways and urge, even compel people to come into His wonderful Kingdom so His house may be filled. We have nothing to lose but everything to gain. The Lord purchased you with His own blood. He held nothing back, so why would you hold back? Throw yourself into His loving arms. You are safer there than anywhere else in this big universe without Him.

Jesus loves you far more than you could ever imagine. He wants His life and anointing flowing through you like a river so He can fully fulfill your unique purpose and destiny and touch countless lives through you. Then your eternal rewards will be spectacular (Daniel 12:3). He will be able to sweep entire cities into His Kingdom through His anointing, glory, and power that flows through *you*. But you have to receive it!

Rise Up!

What are you waiting for? Cast all your cares and worries onto Him. He is the only one who really knows what to do with them. You need to treat worry, sin, cares, sickness, and disease like troublesome demons, casting them out in the mighty name of Jesus. Jesus came to Earth so you don't have to carry the burdens of worry, grief, sickness, mental illness . . . the devil and his demons tremble at the power of the name of Jesus. God can and will take care of all your problems when you give them to Him and leave them with Him in faith, trusting Him to deal with every one of them.

So make the decision today: what will you do? Keep living your life with no progress and no advancement? As stagnant waters that collect mosquitoes and algae? No, I know you won't. Rise up! Even if you once accepted the Lord but have become complacent or you have backslidden, let the river of life begin to flow through you once again. When you wait on Him, seeking Him in prayer, God says your youth will be "renewed like the eagle's" (Psalm 103:5b). God is the Master of making up for lost time. He said you will run and not be weary. You will walk and not faint. According to His Word, He will do whatever you can believe Him for.

Rise up, oh man, woman, and child of God! This is your time! ". . . strengthen the hands which hang down, and the feeble knees . . ." (Hebrews

12:12). Lift up those arms in praise and worship to your King, and you will be revived again. Scripture tells us Abraham of old did not waver at the promise of God:

> [20] He (Abraham) did not waver at the promise of God through unbelief, but was strengthened in faith, giving glory to God, [21] and being fully convinced that what He had promised He was also able to perform. Romans 4:20-21 (my addition in parentheses)

You can do it too! Learn to hear the voice of your King. The One who calms the raging sea. The One who brings fine rain and dew to the lilies. Spend time in prayer before Him, and let Him speak to you in your weariness. Trust Him in the steps you take! Let your God lead you to greener pastures, taking you in His arms and comforting you.

When you decide to stand up and be counted, you will immediately touch others around you, opening the door for God's increased blessings in your life. You have Jesus' love and compassion within you now, but it may not come out unless you allow it to. Like a dam wall, you may have barricaded yourself behind pain and discouragement, and now it's hard for His love to flow. You have imprisoned yourself. Break out of your prison today! Use the TNT of the Holy Spirit, the miracle-working power within you, to blast open that dam wall. Then the torrents of Godly love, power, and hope will surge back into your life and through your life. You can do it. Do it *now*!

Make a daily discipline of being strengthened in the Lord by prayer, and build yourself up by meditating on His Word. Find scriptures that promise solutions to what you need and memorize them. Get them into your heart, speak them daily, and watch the miracle take place. Trust in what you are doing for God; believe that it will carry you through every dark time you may face. Courage isn't the absence of fear—it is moving forward despite being afraid. So be courageous in your weakness. Stand firm in Him. He will see you through.

The Lord wants us to thirst for Him daily as the deer pants for water after a long, hot, dry day. Meditate on that cool drink of His Word and presence to wash away the dryness of your soul's trials. The Lord desires His people to drink deeply of His refreshing mercy and grace. Drink deeply of His Spirit, so when others are in a dry and weary place, living waters will flow from you, filling them as He has filled you. Glory to our awesome God!

Chapter Seven

Bold Evangelism

One of my favorite scriptures, and indeed, a bedrock of my half a lifetime of ministry, is Acts 4:13. This scripture implies anyone can be as bold as Jesus and do even greater works than He did in His limited three years on Earth: "Now when they saw the boldness of Peter and John, and perceived that they were uneducated and untrained men, they marveled. And they realized that they had been with Jesus."

Just before this incident, Peter and John had seen a lame man sitting at the temple gate called "Beautiful," so they brought healing to him through the name of Jesus (Acts 3:1-6). Can you believe the religious leaders quickly had Peter and John arrested and continued persecuting the disciples of the Lord because the truth threatened their corrupt practices as they clung to power over God?

The *name of Jesus* was fundamental to this miracle that took place. It was the core of the miraculous power, and this is the point I want to bring to your attention. The man, who was forty years old, had been lame from birth. On several different occasions, the religious leaders threatened the disciples, whipped them, locked them in prison, and warned them not to preach or teach in the name of Jesus. Why? Because they knew the name of Jesus held the power to create miracles. They *knew* this name carried great power, and they were terrified at even the whisper of Jesus' name because it threatened their corrupt authority, so they commanded the apostles not to preach or teach in this name (Acts 4:17 and Acts 5:28).

The disciples, however, had walked with Jesus. They had known Him personally and had lived with His name on their lips, so they weren't about to obey men over God. While walking the Earth, Jesus said to His disciples, "I will not leave you orphans; I will come to you" (John 14:18), and this was in reference to sending His Holy Spirit, who would empower all of us to use our legal authority as Heaven's royal heirs (Romans 8:17).

Walking close to Jesus and experiencing His power, authority, and boldness will give you a more profound respect and appreciation for His name—it is second to none. Jesus' name is a legal signet that carries the full authority of Heaven, and He gave it to you (Luke 10:19). With the power of the Holy Spirit and their growing knowledge of the authority in their Master's name, the apostles grew in boldness as they developed their faith in Jesus. Do you remember how most of them ran, deserting Him in the garden of Gethsemane when the Roman soldiers came to arrest Him? Only Peter tried to stop them, but even he denied Jesus later that evening. With the name of Jesus in their mouths, nothing could stop the disciples. The more religious leaders persecuted them, the bolder these men and women became.

My friend, the Holy Spirit within you is *all* the power and boldness you need to carry out this good news of the gospel.

These religious leaders are the very same ones who cried out to have Jesus Christ crucified. These leaders have a form of godliness but deny its power (2 Timothy 3:5). This is because the religious traditions of men that are not found in the Word of God nullify the Word of God—there is no miracle-working power in empty rituals, only men's traditions meant to control the people.

The tradition of men consists of doing the same thing continuously, time after time, which effectively becomes a mindless habit with no heartfelt intention behind it, resulting in God's Word having no effect. Jesus says in Mark 7:13,

"Making the word of God of no effect through your tradition which you have handed down. And many such things you do."

On the other hand, a born-again Christian has an active, living relationship with Jesus and does not follow mindlessly manmade traditions. Our Master and King has given us authority and ability, and nothing can stand in our way if we stay obedient to His command: "Behold, I give you the authority to trample on serpents and scorpions, and over all the power of the enemy, and nothing shall by any means hurt you" (Luke 10:19).

These bold New Testament acts of the apostles are a great encouragement to us today, especially concerning the freedom of speech they exercised in the face of religious and political adversity. Unfortunately, we are witnessing similar adversity take place in the USA today. Many political leaders are hell-bent on trying to stop born-again Christian believers from speaking the truth. They are desperately trying to shut us up so they can further their corrupt agenda, but the boldness we have in using the name of Jesus is our defense and our victory, and they will *never* be able to shut us up or shut us down.

I could tell you so many stories about how being bold and using the name of Jesus delivered me and several of my team members from dangerous and difficult situations while preaching in the streets of Johannesburg and several other cities in South Africa over a period of thirteen years. In Acts 4:13, speaking of the boldness of Peter and John, the Greek word *parrhēsía*[4] means "all outspokenness, i.e., frankness, bluntness, publicity; by implication, assurance:—boldly, boldness, boldness of speech), confidence, freely, openly, plainly(-ness). In other words, "bold" in this context means freedom of speech or free utterance of speech.

When I started preaching in the streets of Johannesburg and Hillbrow, the Lord told me to make a wooden cross, a whip, crucifixion nails, and a crown of thorns like the one set on Jesus' head. As I've mentioned, these were used as visual aids to demonstrate the power of the gospel, as people retain a visual aid seventy percent more than just hearing a message. I also stenciled scriptures onto three-inch cardboard strips and stuck them to the cross with putty. Small squares of paper with my message printed on them were also handed out so people could read what I was saying and then take the printed message home to study the Word of God at their convenience. People accepted these messages gratefully and were excited to hear the gospel. Even though I preached in English, I usually had one or two men interpreting my message in local African languages. For many, their Saturday lunch break in downtown Johannesburg became like a regular church service they attended. As I've mentioned, we saw hundreds of thousands of lives changed with these methods, walking in the boldness of Christ.

Apart from preaching, we handed out gospel tracts and books to people—written in their own language—and sent out a bi-monthly newspaper across the country called The Eagle News. Our home church also arranged to have buses running throughout Johannesburg and Hillbrow that the poorer communities could use at no cost.

Often, while we were praising and worshiping God in the open air before I preached, a syndicate of gangsters would hustle and draw people into their gambling games on the outskirts of the crowd we had drawn. The leader often stared at me, but he would never come forward to accept Jesus as his Lord and Savior. Over time these men grew more audacious, mingling with the crowd and gambling in their midst. This soon led to pickpocketing and snatching women's purses. If any of our team tried to intervene, other members of the crew would block the way to prevent their capture. They also played card games, ripping people off right in front of us, disrespecting the presence of God. This infuriated me.

My anger was always aimed at the devil, knowing these unsubtle interruptions were his way of distracting people from salvation. The Bible encourages us to recognize the devil's pernicious schemes: "lest Satan should take advantage of us; for we are not ignorant of his devices" (2 Corinthians 2:11).

Having been set free from a world of extreme violence, I now recognize thugs and troublemakers a long way off. On one particular Saturday morning, the leader of this gang, a stoutly-set man who was stocky and broad in the shoulders, decided to make his most brazen move yet. He brought his mob of gangsters to gamble right at the foot of the cross as I preached. They literally threw dice on the stand holding up the cross, much like the Roman soldiers did before Jesus' cross 2,000 years ago. This was the breaking point for me—I could not stand idle at their disrespect of the cross.

There were hundreds of African people before me, listening intently to the gospel of Christ. They watched the gangsters' actions closely, and I knew the leader was testing me. His gang had also gathered around the people, calling away sections of the crowd to distract them from hearing the gospel.

As I've mentioned, a powerful scripture we can all rely on when being tested by satanic forces is James 4:7: "Therefore submit to God. Resist the devil and he will flee from you." You must be in submission to God, though, because if you are not, the enemy will *not* flee from you when you resist him. This is an important caveat to bear in mind. It is vital that we always walk in submission to God!

I walked over to the gang's leader, and when I got close to him, it was as if I were looking death in the face. His eyes, icy and menacing, seemed to stare right through me. Full of the Spirit of God,

I wasn't fazed. I addressed him directly, speaking loudly enough for those nearby to hear me. I said, "You have all the streets of Johannesburg where you can gamble. Why do you come to the cross to gamble?" He stood up and walked straight toward me, not taking his eyes off mine as he approached.

It became clear he had been waiting for some kind of confrontation with me, as he did not hesitate. Without saying a word, he punched me square in the chest with all his strength. Despite my boxing experience in my younger days, it still took me by surprise. I had been ministering in this area for a number of years, and I had gained great respect from many people who would bring their Bibles and sit on the concrete planters to listen to me and my team preach. I was shocked at his brazen attack on a man bearing the Word of God.

The crowd gasped collectively—they were as shocked as I was. The gangster clenched his fist again, and with another wicked grin and a glint of glee in his eyes, he hit me again . . . but despite his size and the power of his punch, I barely moved. It was his turn to be surprised. He thought he would drop me. The crowd gasped again.

Feeling like he'd been shown up, the gangster wound up to hit me for the third time. Then these words came bellowing out of my mouth, "IN THE *NAME OF JESUS*, YOU WILL NOT LIFT YOUR HAND TO ME AGAIN!"

In mid-swing, the man's entire body froze.

The astonishment on his face was evident for everyone to see. Despite leaning into the punch, being fully in motion mid-swing, his right hand clenched into a vicious fist, the man was locked in that position, unable to move. The name of Jesus stopped him as if he had been instantly frozen. He stuck to the floor in the stance of a shadow boxer attempting to punch the city air. The incident was over. I won by a freeze-out . . . or more precisely, the Lord did. The crowd roared, shouting and rejoicing to see this thug contained by the power of the name of Jesus Christ. The people knew full well these gangsters were not only after me and my team, who preached against their wickedness, but they were also after the people's money and goods.

All I had left to do was call for people to accept Jesus as their personal Lord and Savior, which I did. Hundreds saw what happened, and many rushed forward to accept Christ. As the people prayed and received eternal life, the gang leader remained frozen in that striking stance.

After leading people in the prayer of salvation, we immediately gave them the opportunity to be baptized into the Holy Spirit. After years of ministry experience, I realized that if you don't pray for people to be baptized into the Holy Spirit immediately (or reasonably soon) after receiving Christ, it seems more difficult to receive the infilling of the Spirit of God. I believe there are several reasons for this. Firstly, the enemy is quick to lie to newborn Christians, telling them they are speaking gibberish or, even worse, that speaking tongues is of the devil. How ironic that he would use this tactic against new believers. Sometimes family and friends—or even the church these newborn believers attend—may tell them that speaking in tongues or, rather, praying as the Holy Spirit gives you utterance is of the devil and not of God. Some people may also discourage them by saying baptism into the Holy Spirit ended on the day of Pentecost. This is known as cessation—the belief that the gifts and evidence of the scriptural baptism into the Holy Spirit somehow mysteriously ceased at some random point in the early Church days. It is a lie with zero biblical foundation.

The perpetuation of these lies is why the global Church is largely powerless while Satan is taking increasingly brazen control of the world. This is why I encouraged you to pray for the infilling of the Holy Spirit right after praying the prayer of salvation.

The best thing you can do to remain strong in the Lord is to start sharing your testimony, and the Holy Spirit is the one who empowers you and gives you the ability to do so. For those who would become bold in their evangelism, knowing *how* we stand our ground against the devil's tactics is necessary. Going back to James 4:7—regarding resisting the devil, the word "resist" means "to exert force in opposition[5]" or "to exert oneself so as to counteract or defeat[6]" the resisted temptation. It means we must stand against, oppose, or withstand the enemy so he will flee in stark terror.

Without hesitation and with all sincerity, I can say that the Lord has turned me into an extremely bold person, far beyond what I could ever have imagined. When I first came to Christ, I was depressed, suicidal, dependent on drugs and alcohol, and utterly intimidated by even the quietest person. I could not have walked another step further without God's help. Since the Lord came into my kitchen and my life on that bright, sunny day more than forty years ago, I have never been the same man and will never be the same again. I give my Lord and Savior, Jesus Christ, all the glory.

The first message I ever preached was on July 18, 1981. Exactly thirty-six years later, on the very same day, July 18, 2017, while I was studying the Word, I heard the Lord say to me, "A new boldness is coming upon the body of Christ, the likes of which you have never seen. It will supersede the boldness displayed by the Old Testament prophets and the New Testament apostles."

This has already begun to unfold worldwide. I often receive messages from Bible students and people who went out into the city square with our street-preaching team telling me they are currently ministering in the streets just as we did so many years ago. Nothing blesses me more than to hear this, and it is a great testament to their boldness:

"The wicked flee when no one pursues, But the righteous are bold as a lion" (Proverbs 28:1).

Thank you for reading this book! I pray if you were not a believer in Jesus, my testimony has shown you He can save and use literally anyone. Most of all, I hope it led you to pray the prayer of salvation. It doesn't matter what you've done or how lost you are—you *can* be saved. If you prayed the prayer, I cannot tell you how joyful this makes me. But I don't need to—I believe you're experiencing that joy right now!

If you are a Christian but perhaps are becoming lukewarm in your faith, maybe a little complacent or even backsliding—I pray this book encourages you to turn away from your complacency and reignites the fire of God in your heart. Keep reading the Bible, keep praying, keep hanging out with believers, and keep sharing your testimony, for in doing these, you will keep your fire burning strong.

Scriptures to Read

I encourage you to begin reading your Bible from the book of John in the New Testament. Read the book of Acts next—we are living now in this book called the Acts of the Holy Spirit. Also, find a church that preaches and loves God's holy Word and moves in the power of the Holy Spirit.

May the grace of our Lord Jesus Christ rest upon you all the days of your long and healthy life.

Endnotes

1   Joy, "Paradise Road," 1980, Track 1, Paradise Road, RPM, Vinyl.

2   Revelation 2:11; 20:6; 20:14; and 21:8

3   *mûṯ*. Strong's Hebrew Lexicon, H419

4   *parrhēsía*. Strong's Greek Lexicon, G3954

5   *Merriam-Webster.com Dictionary*, s.v. ."resist," accessed October 4, 2022, https://www.merriam-webster.com/dictionary/resist.

6   Ibid